£2.80

THIS BOOK BELONGS TO...

Daniell Morrall

Printed and Published in Great Britain by D. C. Thomson & Co., Ltd., 185 Fleet Street, London, EC4A 2HS.

But —

DRING!

AAGH!

DRING!

DON'T HANG UP! I'LL BORROW A LONGER LADDER FROM MISTER BROWN.

And —

EEK!

DRING!

HANG ON, MISTER BROWN. I'LL BE BACK IN TWO TICKS.

And —

WHEE! I'M IN!

I HOPE I REACH THE PHONE BEFORE IT STOPS RINGING.

DRING!

But suddenly —

HELP! WHO POLISHED THE FLOOR?

DRING!

AARGH! GROOH!

CRASH!

Then —

IS THAT YOU, GINGER?

I JUST WANTED TO WARN YOU NOT TO DIRTY THE HALL FLOOR. I POLISHED IT JUST BEFORE I LEFT.

GRRR!

What a to-do over a crossword clue!

The NUMSKULLS

Suddenly —

CRASH!

OO-ER! I'LL SEE IF I CAN BRING HIM ROUND.

PAT PAT

GROAN!

Then —

I RECOGNISE THAT SHIRT! IT'S MY MAN! WHEE!

And —

WELCOME BACK, FRED. COME INSIDE.

IT'S GOOD TO BE HOME.

OOH! I HATED JOGGING WITH THAT MAN!

JOGGING! THAT'S THE ANSWER TO OUR MAN'S CROSSWORD. NOW HE CAN GO FOR LUNCH.

_So —_

THAT'S THE CROSSWORD FINISHED. NOW I'LL GO FOR SOMETHING TO EAT.

ALL'S WELL THAT ENDS WELL. THANKS FOR JOGGING MY MEMORY, FRED. HO-HO!

A funny tale about pinching mail!

Just you wait till they open that crate!

The Hillys and the Billys are enjoying their favourite pastime — feuding with each other!

HUH! WE'RE NOT GETTING ANYWHERE JUST FIRIN' AT THE BILLYS' SHACK.

I THINK I'LL MOO-VE!

YEAH! WE HAVE TO GET CLOSER.

BANG! PHOW! BANG!

NOW LET ME SEE! WHAT CAN WE DO?

Suddenly —

I'VE GOT IT! WE COULD GET A LARGE CRATE DELIVERED TO THEM. WE'LL BE INSIDE IT — ARMED TO THE TEETH!

YOU'RE A GENIUS, ZEKE!

Meanwhile —

LET'S GET FERDINAND UNDER COVER.

HE'LL BE SAFE IN THERE. WE CAN GET A LOAD OF FODDER DELIVERED LATER FOR HIM.

That afternoon —

THIS IS FOR YOU.

AH! IT'LL BE FERDINAND'S FEED.

Fairground fun with the saucy one!

COLONEL BLINK
THE SHORT-SIGHTED GINK!

HUH! IT LOOKS LIKE I'LL HAVE TO COOK MY OWN DINNER!

THERE'S FOOD IN THE FRIDGE, BLINKY! I WON'T BE HOME FOR DINNER. AUNTIE

HMM! I'M NOT SURE WHAT I FANCY! LET'S SEE WHAT THERE IS!

YEUCH! FANCY AUNTIE PUTTING AN UNPLUCKED CHICKEN IN THE FRIDGE!

You're in the broom cupboard, Blinky!

BAH! IT'S TIME WE BOUGHT A NEW FRIDGE! THIS ONE ISN'T EVEN COLD!

Later, in town —

AH! THERE'S THE VERY SHOP!

THEY'RE SURE TO HAVE LOTS OF NICE FRIDGES IN HERE!

Puzzle

1. The bill of this bird isn't just for decoration — it's used to burrow into soil to make nests. It can be found on cliff-tops. Is it a (a) Razorbill? (b) Puffin? (c) Fulmar?   *puffin*

2. You're more likely to see this flying monster in a museum than a zoo! It lived millions of years ago in the age of the dinosaurs. Is it a
(a)   Tyrannosaurus?
(b)   Pterodactyl?
(c)   Brontosaurus?

3. Cascading down the hillside for over two hundred feet, this is one of the highest waterfalls in Britain. It's in the Tweedsmuir Hills, near Moffat in Dumfriesshire. Is it the (a) Grey Mare's Tail? (b) Victoria Falls? (c) Falls Of Garry?

4. In gardens throughout Britain, this moth is very common. Its caterpillars, known as "woolly bears", feed on dandelions and other weeds. Is it a (a) Hawk moth? (b) Gypsy moth? (c) Tiger moth?

5. These Chinese are working in a flooded paddy field, helping to produce one of the most important cereal crops in the world. What are they planting? (a) Water cress? (b) Rice? (c) Wheat?   *rice*

Pics

7. During their occupation of Britain, the Romans built many roads. This one ran between Dover and Chester and parts of it are still in use. Is it known as (a) Watling Street? (b) Sauchiehall Street? (c) Downing Street?

6. This colourful amphibian can be found in ponds and pools around Britain. Is it a (a) Salamander? (b) Crested newt? (c) Spotted lizard?

9. This silvery-barked tree is found all over Britain. It is sometimes known as "The Lady Of The Woods". Is it the (a) Beech? (b) Sycamore? (c) Birch?

8. No doubt you'll recognise this as an Indian elephant, but do you know what its rider is called? (a) a Mahout? (b) a Madras? (c) a Howdah?

ANSWERS

1.(b) 2.(b) 3.(a) 4.(c) 5.(b) 6.(b) 7.(a) 8.(a) 9.(c)

YOUNG ★ SID ★

THE COPPER'S KID

I'VE BEEN HAVING GREAT FUN WITH THIS SLIDE!

NOW I'LL BUILD MYSELF A SMASHING SNOWMAN.

Soon after—

SEARCHING FOR BERNARD, THE BURGLAR, IS COLD WORK. I CAN'T WAIT TO NIP INDOORS AND WARM UP BY THE FIRE.

PLOOF!

HEY! MIND MY SNOWMAN!

BAH! BUILDING IT SO NEAR THE GATE WAS PRETTY SILLY. I COULDN'T SEE IT FOR THE TREE.

I GUESS DAD'S RIGHT! I'VE BUILT ANOTHER SNOWMAN IN THE BACK GARDEN.

Meanwhile, inside—

I'LL NEED SOME MORE COAL.

THE BANANA BUNCH

CHOO-CHOO! CHUG-A-CHUG-A!

THIS IS A SMASHING FILM!

But then—

OOPS! SORRY, BRAINY!

'BUMP!

AARGH!

WHACK!

YELP!

YOU CLUMSY FOOL! YOU RAN OVER BRAINY'S FOOT WITH YOUR STUPID TRAIN!

GRRR! PLAY WITH SOMETHING LESS DANGEROUS!

GROWL!

And so—

I CAN'T INJURE ANYONE WITH MY PAPER AEROPLANE!

Now he's here! Now he's not! That very funny tiny tot!

Baby Crockett

ONE DAY, ME'LL BE ABLE TO SEE IN THE MIRROR WITHOUT JUMPING UP AND DOWN!

HUNGRY HOSS

Then— BUZZ

This scruffy lad drives Mum mad!

SMIFFY

I'LL HAVE A CAN OF ORANGE JUICE WHILE I READ MY BEEZER.

But—

OH, NO!

WHOOSH

I'VE STAINED THE WALLPAPER. I'D BETTER COVER IT UP BEFORE MUM SEES IT.

HMM! THIS POSTER'S TOO SMALL!

UNITED

MAYBE THIS ONE WILL COVER THE STAIN!

OH, NO! THAT'S NO GOOD EITHER!

PAW, MAW and PORKY

Baby Crockett

OOH! IT'S BATH NIGHT! HOW CAN ME GET OUT OF IT?

AHA! ME KNOWS!

HEE-HEE!

Soon after—

IT'S TIME TO RUN BABY'S BATH.

Suddenly—

SCREAM!

THERE'S A HORRIBLE SPIDER IN THE BATH.

MY RUBBER SPIDER SCARED MUM.

Just then—

OO-ER!

HELP!

OUR SHERIFF'S AN APE!

COYOTE CREEK is one of the most peaceful towns in the Wild West — and no wonder! It has two sheriffs! One is a normal sort of bloke called Danny Blain — but the other is a huge ape called Charlie!

THERE'S CHARLIE — EATING BANANAS AS USUAL, DAVE.

Suddenly —

YAHOO! I'M WILDCAT WEBSTER, THE TERROR OF THE TERRITORY. I'M ON THE PROWL AND THIS IS MY DAY TO HOWL!

SHERIFF

HUH?

EEK!

HELP!

It certainly was Wildcat's day to howl — especially when Charlie swept some banana skins in front of his horse!

WAAGH!

HEE-HEE!

Then —

SPLOOSH!

HO-HO! WILDCAT LOOKS MORE LIKE A WET FISH!

HUH-HUH!

CAFE

LET THAT BE A LESSON TO YOU. WE LIKE TO KEEP THIS TOWN QUIET.

GRR!

Soon after —

OLD CHARLIE'S GOING TO SLEEP.

HO-HO! WELL, LET'S CATCH HIM NAPPING, PETE!

Next second, Charlie got a rude awakening!

OW!

WHEE! WHAT A SHOT!

The big ape didn't like anybody making a monkey of him — so he chucked the orange back at the youngsters!

CAFE

DUCK, DAVE.

WOW!

Meanwhile, Wildcat Webster was in a nearby café.

I'M STARVING! I CAN'T WAIT TO GET STUCK INTO THIS GRUB.

He got stuck into his food quicker than he thought!

OOMPH!

The bean-covered billy rushed outside and saw Dave with the oranges!

SO YOU FIRED THAT ORANGE AT ME, EH? COME HERE!

WAAGH! WE DIDN'T DO ANYTHING.

It looked as if the youngsters were going to get a real thrashing. Then Wildcat felt a tap on his shoulder.

WHAT . . . ?

When he turned round —

GRR!

OO-ER! I WAS JUST— ER — JOKING! RUN ALONG, NICE CHILDREN!

Then —

DON'T BE MAD AT US, CHARLIE. WE DIDN'T MEAN TO HIT YOU. IT WAS — ER — AN ACCIDENT.

Charlie reckoned that the boys needed some catapult practice. He made them follow him to a bit of waste land behind some buildings.

WHAT'S HE GOING TO DO, PETE?

I DON'T KNOW, BUT I THINK HE BELIEVED ME WHEN I SAID IT WAS AN ACCIDENT.

The hairy sheriff set up a proper shooting gallery for the young pals.

WOW! THIS IS A GREAT IDEA, CHARLIE.

It must have been a fluke that Dave managed to hit Charlie. The youngsters certainly couldn't knock any of the cans off the fence.

The big ape grabbed Dave's catapult! He would show the kids how to do it!

He took careful aim and pulled back the elastic.

CRACK! The catapult suddenly snapped!

A stronger catapult was required — and Charlie found the very thing to make one nearby.

Soon, a pair of old braces and a bit of drainpipe became a king-sized catapult.

Once more, the hairy sheriff took aim.

CRUMP! Charlie hit the fence — and it went over as if it were made of paper!

AAIIEE!

WHAT WAS THAT?

The falling fence had flattened Wildcat Webster!

HUH?

WHAT HIT ME? OOH!

YOU OUGHT TO BE LOCKED UP, YOU MENACE!

WE'RE LEAVING! YOU'RE MORE DANGEROUS THAN US WITH A CATAPULT!

Later —

THERE'S A BIG REWARD FOR THIS BOUNDER.

HM!

WANTED

Soon after, another kind of "bounder" came hopping out of the bank. He was the manager and he was bound up like a trussed chicken!

HUH!

WOW! WHAT'S BEEN GOING ON?

BANK

I'VE BEEN ROBBED, SHERIFF BLAIN.

TELL ME WHAT HAPPENED!

LET'S GO INTO THE BANK AND TAKE A LOOK.

HM?

Then —

Danny Blain got a big surprise when Charlie suddenly grabbed him and dragged him round to the back of the bank!

HOI! WHERE ARE WE GOING? LEAVE ME ALONE.

HELLO, CHARLIE! COMING BACK FOR SOME MORE PRACTICE?

The corn in the bank had puzzled Danny but, when Charlie's pals explained that Wildcat had been flattened by the fence round the cornfield, it all became clear!

So —

YOU LEFT BITS OF CORN ALL OVER THE BANK WHEN YOU RAIDED IT! YOU'RE UNDER ARREST!

HUH!

But Webster hadn't got his nickname for nothing! He leapt to his feet like a wildcat and —

WAGH!

UGH!

And then —

The big ape dived for cover behind a rock.

Charlie had only one weapon with him — his catapult! He picked up a rock . . .

. . . and let fly!

But then —

With loose shale and rocks falling all around him, the bank-raider took to his heels!

But then he ran into a brick wall — or, at least, it felt like it!

OOF!

When Charlie arrived back in town —

WELL DONE, CHARLIE. YOU CAUGHT HIM!

YOU DESERVE A REWARD. I'LL GIVE YOU FREE BANANAS FOR A MONTH.

Ho-ho-ho! Hats off to Mo!

What a hoot when Hoss gets the boot!

HUNGRY HOSS

Then—

AAAIEEE!

THAT'S FUNNY! I THINK I HEAR A SCREAM!

Miles out of town—

GRR! WAIT TILL I GET MY HANDS ON WHOEVER DID THIS!

Meanwhile, in town—

WAIT OUT HERE WHILE I GET THE CASH, HOSS!

But—

I'M NOT STAYING. I'M HUNGRY. I'LL LOOK FOR SOME GRUB.

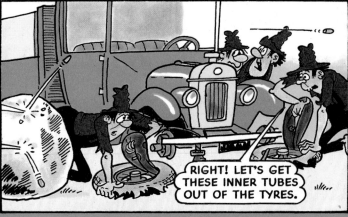

BEEZER

1 — Mo is mixing together a spider, an owl, a bat, a fish, a toad and a newt in her witch's cauldron. Take one letter from each of these ingredients to find out what she's making.

2 — There are 10 differences between these two spooky pictures. See if you can spot them.

3 — Blinky thinks these 4 headless ghosts all look the same, but only 2 are, in fact, identical. Can you spot them?

TEEZERS

4 — The patterns on the wall panels change from left to right. Ginger can't work out what the pattern on the fourth panel should be. Can you?

5 — There are 6 Numskulls hidden on these pages. See if you can find them.

SCARE

1. share
2. shark
3. shack

SHOCK

6 — Poor Baby Crockett's had a terrible shock. He's just seen a scary ghost. Turn SCARE into SHOCK in four steps, changing one letter each time to form a new word.

ANSWERS

1. Mo is making a POTION.

2. Window is missing on castle; Flag different; Ghost missing; Crow instead of bat; Trees missing; No clouds across moon; Spike missing on P.C. 99's helmet; His tie is missing; His hand is missing; Sid's socks are different colours.

3. 2 and 3 are identical.

4.

5. Behind candle on wall above Pop; In mousehole beside Pop; Behind Blinky's brolly; Near ghost on stair landing; Beside spider; Behind right hand picture on wall.

6. Scare; Share; Shark; Shack; Shock.

SCRAPPER

YOUNG SID

THE COPPER'S KID

Then—

And—

A crazy caper with miles of paper!

THE BADD LADS

Early one morning—

LOOK! A NEWSAGENT'S NEWSPAPERS!

YEAH! WE CAN SELL THOSE!

JUST WAITING TO BE NICKED.

BUY A BEEZER

A quick nick later—

READ ALL ABOUT IT!

THANK YOU, SIR!

HEY! THIS IS YESTERDAY'S PAPER!

SO IS THIS!

GRR! CHEAT US WITH OLD NEWSPAPERS, EH?

THUMP!

HUH! THE BIN MEN MUST'VE COME EARLY THIS MORNING. I HAD MORE PAPERS TO BE LIFTED!

Back at the hideout—

MILLIONAIRE INKWELL PENN PUBLISHES NEW PAPER

IF WE COULD PRINT OUR OWN PAPER WE COULD BECOME MILLIONAIRES!

CAVIAR BUTTIES

SOLID GOLD

BUT WE'D NEED A PRINTING PRESS.

THERE'S A PRINTING SET IN KNUCK'S OLD TOY BOX!

And so—

START PRINTING!

THIS IS FUN!

THUMP!

SPLOSH!

THUMP!

HOW DOES THAT LOOK?

IT'S NOT QUITE RIGHT, SOMEHOW.

NEWZ WEE BRING YEW YESTERDAYS NOOZ. TUM ORRAH

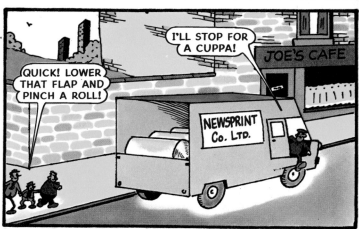

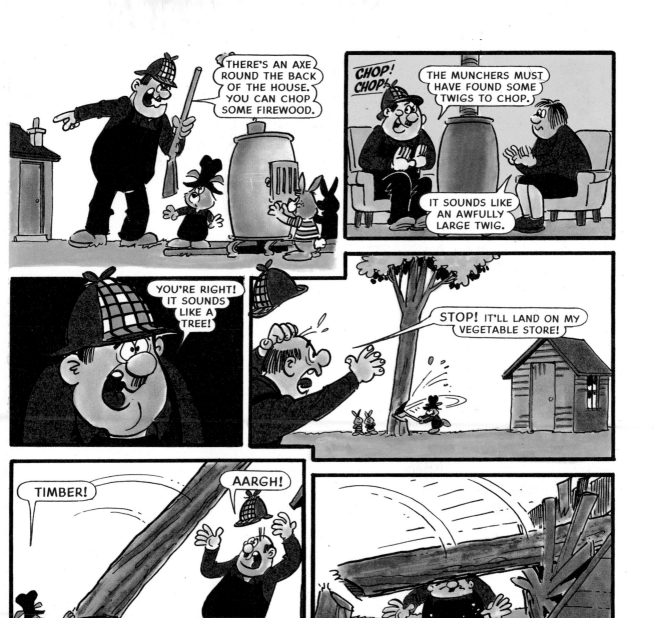

Good grief! A flying thief!

GINGER

BAH! I'M BROKE AS USUAL.

HEY! MONEY! THIS IS MY LUCKY DAY. I'LL BE ABLE TO BUY SWEETS WITH THAT.

HM! MAYBE I SHOULD HAND IT IN TO THE POLICE.

I'LL TOSS TO DECIDE!

Suddenly—

WAAGH! A THIEVING MAGPIE!

COME BACK WITH THAT COIN!

Then—

HO-HO! OOPS!

CRUMP!

OOYAH!

Then—

WHAT WAS THAT?

DID THAT BIRD DROP SOMETHING ONTO MY HAT?

WOW! IT'S LANDED ON THAT SPADE. THANK GOODNESS IT DIDN'T GO INTO THE FIRE.

EXCUSE ME! THIS IS MY COIN.

CAREFUL!

WAAGH! IT'S RED HOT!

I DID TRY TO WARN YOU!

SIZZLE

EEK! IT'S GONE DOWN A DRAIN.

PLOP!

JOE BROWN was known as Joe Soap by the people in Sudbury. You see, he was always blowing amazing bubbles made by his grandfather, a real crackpot inventor.

WHERE'S JOE? HE'S ALWAYS LATE FOR HIS LUNCH!

WELL, WE WON'T WAIT. HE CAN EAT HIS COLD!

Later—

THERE YOU ARE AT LAST. YOUR LUNCH IS COLD!

IT'LL MAYBE TEACH YOU TO BE ON TIME FOR MEALS.

GROOH! THIS IS AWFUL, GRANDAD!

NEVER MIND, JOE. I HAVE SOMETHING THAT'LL STOP YOU BEING LATE AGAIN.

And in the garden shed —

I'VE INVENTED SOME BUBBLE MIXTURE THAT'LL MAKE YOU A GOOD TIME-KEEPER.

OO-ER! I DON'T LIKE THE SOUND OF THAT.

EEK! I'M OFF!

Double trouble with a pin and a flying litter bin!

SMIFFY

WHO'S THIS, I WONDER. THAT'S A REAL FANCY CAR!

TIDY TOWN COMPETITION

We want our town to win SO KEEP IT TIDY

Councillor Scrubby

I'M COUNCILLOR SCRUBBY! BE A GOOD BOY AND PUT THIS IN THE CORNER OF THAT POSTER.

TIDY TOWN COMPETITION We want our town to win SO KEEP IT

OKAY, MISTER!

HOLD IT! WIPE THE MUD OFF YOUR HANDS FIRST.

HUH!

THERE! IS THAT BETTER?

WIPE

WAAH! NOT ON MY CAR, YOU FOOL! DON'T YOU HAVE A HANDKERCHIEF?

HMM! I'VE GOT ONE SOMEWHERE!

AH! HERE IT IS!

The fun sure is good — with Pop's favourite food!

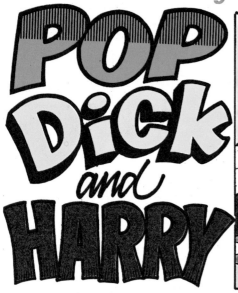

OH, WELL! ONE'S BETTER THAN NOTHING!

GRR! I'LL BET THE TWINS DID THAT!

GIVE ME THIS PESKY BOW AND ARROW!

THERE! THAT'LL PUT A STOP TO ANY MORE NONSENSE!

BAH! WHAT A ROTTER!

Soon after —

HELLO! COULD I ORDER A POUND OF SAUSAGES FOR LUNCHTIME, PLEASE?

Meanwhile —

WE CAN MAKE NEW BOWS AND ARROWS WITH THESE CANES, DICK.

GOOD IDEA!

Later, in the garden —

HM! I SHOULD PROP UP THOSE FLOWERS WITH CANES.

But, in the shed —

HEY! WHERE HAVE MY CANES GONE?

Then —

THUD!

THUD!

WHAT'S THAT NOISE? I'LL TAKE A LOOK!

AHA! SO **THIS** IS WHERE MY CANES HAVE GOT TO!

A ball full of tricks lands the Bunch in a fix!

THE BANANA BUNCH

HUNGRY HOSS

Well, fancy that! Mo's laid Mugsy flat!